CW00602404

CHRISTCHURCH
Botanic Gardens

DENISE HUNTER

Designed, published and printed by

THE CAXTON PRESS
P R I N T & D E S I G N

CHRISTCHURCH, NEW ZEALAND
www.caxton.co.nz

"The Botanic Gardens

remains for me a sanctuary and a living,
breathing future paradise of inspiration for
everyone to enjoy. "
                                    – MARK HADLOW

© Liz Clark

From the
Curator

Some of the world's most famous botanic gardens were established centuries ago. They have stood the test of time by staying true to their principles of collecting, conserving and studying their plants, while adapting to the needs of the public or institutions that support them. Today, botanic gardens are much more than walled paradises for the rich and their physicians; they are popular places of display, delight and exploration.

The Christchurch Botanic Gardens are not ancient but we are still famous for our landscape, our trees, our gorgeous, sometimes quirky, floral displays, and a proud record of conservation of New Zealand's indigenous flora, research and education. And while our Botanic Gardens are full of plant collections and their teeming biodiversity of bees and butterflies above and fungi and bacteria below, we also have more than a million people visiting annually. It is the people that we welcome, people who come to relax or pass the time of day, and who might learn something about the world around them while they are here.

The book reminds me of some of the Gardens' most secret places of sanctuary and personal memories, but also of the brassy, sunny places, ice creams and entertainment. Staff of the Christchurch Botanic Gardens will continue to conserve the collections and work hard to serve your needs into the future as the green heart of the wider parks network of Christchurch, a true garden city within the productive and wild landscapes of Canterbury.

John Clemens
Curator

Contents

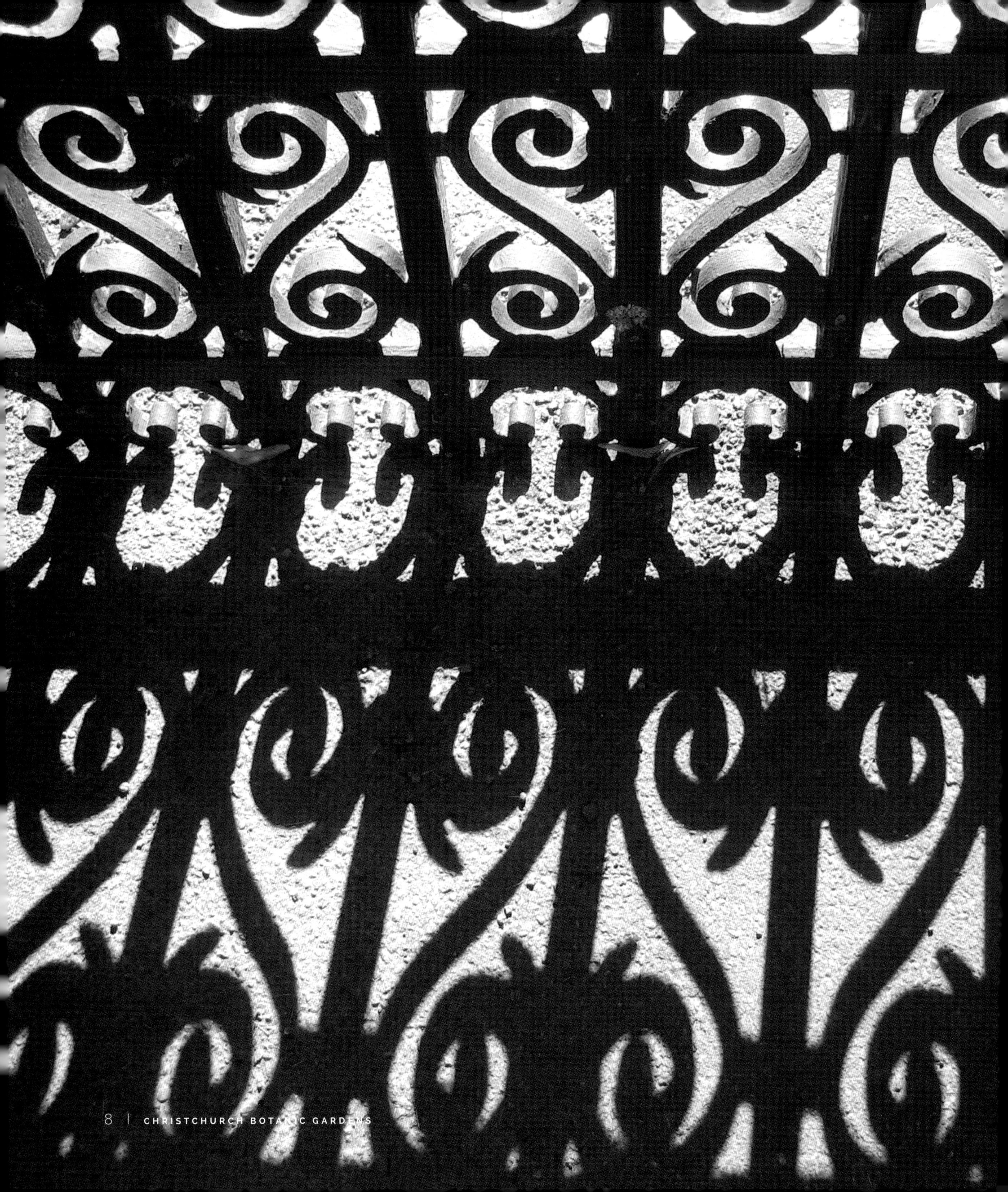

© Priscilla Chapman

The *Inspiration*

When the September 2010 and February 2011 earthquakes, and the subsequent aftershocks, temporarily brought Christchurch to its knees, there was one significant oasis that many Cantabrians turned to for a connection with 'normality', a place of calm serenity, and a land and skyscape that was largely left unscathed – the Christchurch Botanic Gardens.

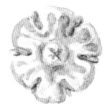

The Gardens provided a sense of strength, a promise that life could return to normal, and those who sought its peace and beauty were reassured and inspired in a city that was otherwise in turmoil. One of those who was drawn to reconnect with this serene garden setting was local artist Denise Hunter.

Driving from the East through a shaken city with broken roads, newly erected security fences, detours, road cones and tumbled buildings on her way to work in Riccarton, Denise couldn't help but appreciate the natural beauty of Hagley Park and the Botanic Gardens at its heart. She sensed its healing power and one day stopped her car and wandered along the winding pathways. She found herself spending more and more time in the Gardens which reflect 150 years of the city's proud history. The beauty inspired her, the trees drew her attention. She began photographing her favourite places. She started drawing and painting trees and various species' leaves – focussing on the minutiae that build from the tiniest fragments of nature to become a complete majestic garden exhibit.

Denise's photography and art have combined to present this visual meander through the Christchurch Botanic Gardens, capturing the aesthetic beauty as well as the calm ambiance of this special place that is a treasure of Christchurch.

© Liz Clark

The History & *Nature*

Mighty oaks from little acorns grow.

When Government Gardener Enoch Barker planted the
Albert Edward oak on 9 July 1863, he had little idea that this
would be the foundation of a botanic garden that, 150 years
later, attracts more than one million visitors each year.

From fields used for pasturing cattle, visionary gardeners created a Botanic Garden of striking trees, flamboyant flowers, surprising plant collections, meandering paths and contemplative spaces which each have their strengths and unique beauty at varying times of the day and in contrasting seasons.

The oak was planted to commemorate the wedding of Queen Victoria's son Albert Edward, Prince of Wales, to Princess Alexandra of Denmark a few months earlier. One delightful (but unproven) story has it that Queen Victoria herself sent the acorn.

The site for a botanical garden had been chosen in 1849 by Captain Joseph Thomas on the "extensive and fertile" plains near Banks Peninsula. In England, the Canterbury Association had been formed in London in 1847 to promote and establish a Church of England settlement in New Zealand. In 1850 the first of the Canterbury Association's ships sailed into the new settlement of Lyttelton with the Canterbury pilgrims on board.

The area that was to become Christchurch had been pegged out with parallel streets, squares and open spaces. A public reserve of approximately five hundred acres was set aside and named Hagley Park after Lord Lyttelton's county seat in Worcestershire – Lord Lyttelton being a founding father of the Canterbury Association.

An ordinance issued by the Canterbury Association in 1855 declared that Hagley Park was to be "open for the recreation and enjoyment of the public". Difficult to imagine now, but in the early days much of the parkland was used for the pasturing of cattle.

In 1862 John Francis Armstrong arrived in New Zealand and was appointed Government Gardener in charge of the Domain, as the Botanic Gardens were called in those days. During his 22 years in this position, he established a large collection of plants and planned many of the pathways and walks. His son Joseph assisted him for 16 years, collecting many native plants from around the country.

During the older Armstrong's time, probably in 1875, the original New Zealand plant section was established.

Fourteen years later, Ambrose Lloyd Taylor arrived in New Zealand. He assisted in planning the avenues of trees and helped with the extensive planting undertaken in both the Botanic Gardens and Hagley Park.

FAR LEFT: Enoch Barker, first Government Gardener, 1860 - 1867. From 1864 he was in charge of the Botanic Gardens. © Christchurch Botanic Gardens

LEFT: J.F. Armstrong, Curator 1867 - 89. © Christchurch Botanic Gardens

BOTTOM LEFT: A.L. Taylor, Curator 1889 - 1907. © Christchurch Botanic Gardens

BELOW: The Canterbury Museum from the Armstrong lawn.
© The Weekly Press photograph, Bishop Collection, Canterbury Museum

Constrained by funding issues, he was unable to carry out all the improvements he had planned.

The Public Domains Act of 1895 describes Hagley Park and the Domain (Botanic Gardens) as 495 acres (200-odd hectares), including 13 acres taken for a public hospital and roads through the park.

The Children's Playground, the Tea Kiosk and four propagating houses were built in the early years of the 20th century, when James Young was curator. In 1913 the Domain was renamed the Botanic Gardens. A very large rose garden was established and two of the Gardens' conservatories, Townend House and Cuningham House, were erected. The rose garden was later redesigned.

In 1946 for financial reasons, an Act to dissolve the Christchurch Domains Board was passed by Parliament, and Hagley Park and the Botanic Gardens were placed under the control of the Christchurch City Council. Later, Morris John Barnett raised a loan of 20,000 pounds to finance, among other construction work, the building of a library and offices for staff.

The second Townend House and Garrick Cactus House were completed with Huia Gilpin, the director of Botanic Gardens, Parks and Reserves, in the 1950s and 1960s.

Soon after, the centenary of the Botanic Gardens in 1963 was marked by the erection of a charming new stone and wrought-iron fence, still in place, along Rolleston Avenue.

The Tea Kiosk, originally built circa 1910, was destroyed by fire in 1922 and rebuilt the following year. That building was again damaged by fire five decades later, in 1979, and rebuilt for the second time using the existing brickwork. The Tea Kiosk became a popular café and meeting place for families, friends and walking groups before being closed after the February 2011 earthquake.

Recent history of the Botanic Gardens has seen Dr John Clemens appointed curator in 2009. The first Canterbury earthquake, in September 2010, resulted in some trees being removed from the Gardens in the interests of public safety.

On 22 February 2011 the earth shuddered with the force of a large, shallow earthquake centred in the Port Hills just south of the city. The results were disastrous, causing far more damage to the entire city and satellite towns. Botanic Gardens' buildings such as the Curator's House, the Tea Kiosk and the conservatories, as well as other structures in the vicinity – the Bandsmen's Memorial Rotunda and the Herbert Memorial – suffered varying degrees of damage. In January 2013 Christchurch City Mayor Bob Parker launched the start of the Botanic Gardens 150th anniversary by officiating the ceremony for the planting of the Wollemi pine. The rare tree, thought to be extinct until 1994, is classified as critically endangered.

The Gardens continue to be enjoyed and appreciated by visitors from around the world.

"One of the great strengths of the Botanic Gardens has been the free accessibility for people from all walks of life. Whether people have an interest in botany, horticulture, conservation or passive leisure, the Gardens have been able to fulfil their needs."

WARWICK SCADDEN, CURATOR 1983 – 1999

Royal plantings

Over the years royal visitors have planted some of the Gardens' most notable trees. The first royal visitor to New Zealand was Prince Alfred Ernest Albert, Duke of Edinburgh, second son of Queen Victoria and Prince Albert. He arrived in Wellington on 11 April 1869 as Captain of HMS Galatea. In Christchurch he visited the Botanic Gardens where he was scheduled to plant an English oak (*Quercus robur*), to be known as Prince Alfred's oak. He apparently enjoyed the experience so much he went on to plant four more trees including a redwood (*Sequoiadendron giganteum*), two species of cedar, and a totara presented by John Armstrong. The redwood is still alive.

Other royal plantings include a kauri (*Agathis australis*) planted by Edward Prince of Wales (later King Edward VII) on 15 May 1920 and a purple Norway maple (*Acer platanoides* 'Goldsworth Purple') by Queen Elizabeth II on 20 January 1954. She also planted an English oak in February 1963 to commemorate the centenary of the Christchurch Botanic Gardens and a tulip tree (*Liriodendron tulipifera*) on 1 March 1986 to mark the occasion of the royal visit.

Centuries of seed exchange

The plant collections are the lifeblood of the Christchurch Botanic Gardens. In the past many exotic collections were built up using an international seed exchange, a system where botanic gardens all over the world cooperated on the collection and exchange of seeds. In this way, they gained access to seeds and grew plants they would otherwise have difficulty obtaining. It has been one way the Gardens obtained new or unusual plants.

The system was quaintly old fashioned, but worked well. The list of collected seeds was named the Index Seminum, Latin for Seed Index, and the order form the desiderata, which translates to desirable things. Thanks to the use of botanical nomenclature - also in Latin - the Index Seminum was published in a common language that could be understood in countries all around the world.

Each botanic garden would annually publish a list of seeds gathered throughout the previous season and this Index Seminum would be sent to participating gardens along with information about the seed. One of the earlier examples of the Index Seminum is from the Hortus Botanicus Amsterdam, which published its first list in 1805. In Christchurch, John Armstrong (pioneering Government Gardener and curator 1867-89) made the first exchange of seeds with Tasmania and Europe in 1881, although the earliest records of the Gardens' involvement in the Index Seminum is 1940.

Nowadays old meets new, with many gardens publishing their Index Seminum and receiving desiderata online. However, past introductions worldwide have led to many examples of devastating weed outbreaks that are costly or impossible to control. As a result, any introductions now conform with biosecurity laws and are carefully monitored for weed contamination .

Botanic gardens now tend to focus on conserving their indigenous floras and habitats, although the legacy of past introductions allows us to enjoy plants from around the world. Some plants introduced from other countries through the Index Seminum network are threatened with extinction in their home countries and these are carefully conserved.

Botanists

Today the Gardens have many thousands of exotic and native plant species.

Importing and tending to these botanical gems was the responsibility of a talented succession of curators, gardeners and botanical enthusiasts.

The first to plant was the government gardener Enoch Barker, a Yorkshire man credited with planting many of the city's most magnificent trees.

Supporting the conservation and display of New Zealand native plants in the Gardens was initially a role taken on by father and son curatorial team John and Joseph Armstrong. They amassed a wonderful collection, later admired by eminent New Zealand scientist Leonard Cockayne, and published many botanical reports and papers before resigning in 1889.

Leonard Cockayne was an avid botanist and horticulturist excited by protecting and promoting the diversity of New Zealand's stunning alpine, forest and wetland flora, as well as helping the Government and the people of New Zealand in practical matters like agriculture, soil conservation, and forestry.

The Cockayne Memorial Garden is dedicated to honouring his devotion to native botanical study.

Botanic Gardens bridges

To give visitors access to the Gardens, three bridges have been built to span the Avon River as it winds its way towards the waters of Pegasus Bay.

To the south, and just near the Bandsmen's Memorial Rotunda, the graceful Woodland Bridge lies close to Riccarton Avenue, offering the best access over the river to the Peace Bell. The area is particularly stunning in spring, when daffodils bloom in their thousands across the Woodland Lawn.

The West Bridge, as its name suggests, is on the western side of the Gardens. A sturdy bridge, it is well used by people entering the Gardens from the car parking area near the tennis courts. It is close to the Azalea and Magnolia Garden.

At the northern side, the Armagh footbridge links the Armagh Street car park with the Gardens and is close to the former Tea Kiosk. It happens to be the closest bridge to the Children's Playground and paddling pool while also the easiest bridge to use for those coming from attractions such as Victoria Lake in Hagley Park.

No bridge is necessary on the eastern side of the Gardens, as access is via Rolleston Avenue. The river makes a detour, looping around this very special place.

NEW ZEALAND SCAUP (PAPANGO)

Birds in the Gardens

These are but a few of the 400 or so species of native and introduced birds that have discovered that the trees and ponds of the Gardens provide them with five-star food and lodging in the central city.

For many generations of children, feeding the ducks in the Avon River and the Kiosk Lake has been a highlight of their earliest visit to the Botanic Gardens. Meander further afield and you may be startled by the slow thwack of the wings of kereru, the native woodpigeon, as it flops clumsily from tree to tree, or be followed by a cheeky pīwakawaka or fantail, eager not for companionship, but by the prospects of insect life disturbed by human movement. You may hear the short repetitive call of the koromako or bellbird, the cheerful non-stop song of the riroriro or grey warbler, and be startled by a flock of tiny green silvereyes. Some live there all year, others, like the little shags, visit seasonally. Every spring, these elegant long necked diving birds build their twiggy nests in the trees around the Kiosk Lake and keep an eye on those mallards, pūtakitaki / paradise ducks, and scaup that busily and bossily criss-cross the pools. These fascinating creatures return to the same nests every year to rear their young, providing entertainment for ornithologists, photographers and the general public alike.

SILVEREYE

A River's Voice

If the Avon could talk,
there'd be more to tell than
of old timers fishing the shallows
sharing tall tales, or,
of crowds once cheering
favoured boatmen.

It would whisper
of lovers' trysts
hidden by willows,
soft grasses crushed
on its sloping banks, or,
murmur
of nurses gently
consoled by a mass
of gold dancing
to the water's edge.

The river might
chuckle at ducklings
chased by squeals, and
squashed crumbs held
tight in tiny fists, or
laugh loudly at
schoolboys' tomfoolery, and
late night revelry.

- Jacqui Wood

Avon River Ōtākaro

Springs flowing from the west of the city once forced a surge of water through swampy lands toward the Pacific Ocean .

Today, the Avon River/Ōtākaro winds at a more leisurely pace framing most of the gardens within its tidal drift.

The river's bed has been altered and its flow slowed over the years. Straightening, widening and deepening was mainly the work of the Christchurch Drainage Board set up in 1875 with the task of flood protection for the burgeoning city.

Originally, the Canterbury Association had planned to call the river Shakespeare, but instead, in 1848, early settler John Deans named it after the River Avon in his homeland of Scotland.

Today, to honour the Ngāi Tahu Claims Settlement Act 1998 its official name is Avon River/Ōtākaro.

The Wind in The Willows by Kenneth Grahame, adapted by Alan Bennett is, to this day, one of my most favourite and rewarding plays. In February 2013, in the Christchurch Botanic Gardens, I got to do my fifth and most enjoyable portrayal of Toady outdoors and on the river. 30,000 people flocked to see 'open air' theatre in the most idyllic setting possible. It doesn't get any better than this; being a Toad, thrashing around on the river bank and being naughty in a motor car or on the water, and having the time of your life. Bliss. I am sure Grahame was imagining the Botanic Gardens when he wrote the story for his son over 100 years ago.

The Botanic Gardens remains for me a sanctuary and a living, breathing future paradise of inspiration for everyone to enjoy.

MARK HADLOW, TOAD, "*WIND IN THE WILLOWS*", 2013

ABOVE: Actor Mark Hadlow reveling in his role as Toad in '*Wind in the Willows*'.

BELOW: '*Wind in the Willows*' on the banks of the Avon River / Ōtākaro.

Weeping willows
Salix babylonica

A pretty myth surrounds the weeping willows that shimmer in the breeze as they overhang the rippling Avon River. They are reported to be descended from the tree at Napoleon's grave on the island of St Helena. One of the early French settlers, who arrived in Akaroa in 1840, is said to have brought a cutting from that tree and planted it in the French Cemetery. Cuttings of the Akaroa tree were supposedly later planted along the Avon. No evidence has come to light to back up this rather charming story, but there's a similar one across the Tasman. The original willow trees in Canberra, Australia, are also reputed to have come from a tree near Napoleon's grave. Once again, the tale is not authenticated.

© Priscilla Chapman

Guide
to the Gardens

The Christchurch Botanic Gardens offer surprisingly different and striking first impressions and an extraordinary selection of vistas depending on your choice of entrance and trail.

In step with your soul's desire you can be met with sweeping lawns and formal gardens, shady woodland hideaways, bright, flourishing blooms, majestic trees, fascinating ancient flora, trickling springs, sparkling rivers crossed by stone bridges warmed in the sun, fragrance that bombards the senses, or a true representation of New Zealand as it used to be.

Enjoy the various collections of the Gardens which are celebrated on the following pages, and take a virtual stroll in your area of interest, or plan what discoveries you will make in your next visit to this inspiring place.

Kate Sheppard Walk

Hall Lawn

18

**GONDWANA &
THE WESTERN END**

Playground

NORTH

Pond

Fern House

16

West Bridge

Magnetic Observatory

14

15

Foweraker House

Cuningham House

**AZALEA
& MAGNOLIA
GARDENS**

13

Botanic Gardens Centre

Rose Garden

Rose Sculpture

Herbaceous Border

Water Garden

10

7

5

CENTRAL GARDENS

9

AVON RIVER

**NEW ZEALAND &
WATER GARDENS**

Fern Sculpture

11

Maple Border

ARCHERY LAWN

Pinetum

6

4

12

Peacebell

Rock Garden

New Zealand Gardens

17

8

The Wrestlers Sculpture

Heather Garden

Woodland Bridge

Cockayne Memorial Garden

AVON RIVER

WOODLANDS

Harman's Grove

Bandsmen's Memorial Rotunda

Heritage Rose Garden

Map
of the Gardens

No two visits to the Christchurch Botanic Gardens are ever the same. Each stroll reveals new areas of interest from trees and plants that have been overlooked in the past, to flowers that have recently come into bloom, or thought provoking sculptures. Each section of the Gardens has its own unique mood and aspects of fascination. Peruse this map to gain an overview of this diverse and extensive Garden and discover pathways that will take you on new invigorating journeys.

Iris Border

Regret Sculpture

Foundry Sculpture

3

2

1

Peacock Fountain

ARMSTRONG LAWN

ROLLESTON AVENUE

Curator's House

Vegetable & Herb Garden

The Armstrong Lawn

Capacious paths, long lawns and formal gardens once played host to royals gracing civic ceremonies, Victorian ladies revealing Sunday finery, and students escaping study from within stony walls. The lawn was named in honour of curator John Armstrong whose most heroic botanical endeavours, along with his son Joseph, were focused on the conservation of the New Zealand flora. Paradoxically, the Armstrong Lawn today is maintained with a cheerful nod to English grandeur.

The Peacock Fountain

First unveiled in June 1911, the Peacock Fountain, beside the Canterbury Museum on Rolleston Avenue, has had a life almost as colourful as its glazings.

Wealthy businessman and politician John Peacock Jnr left a handsome £500 bequest to the Christchurch Beautifying Association in 1905, suggesting the gift be used for 'beautifying the reserves and gardens' and 'improving the River Avon'.

The Association chose to purchase an extraordinary, iron fountain from the most famous of ironworks – Coalbrookdale in Shropshire, England.

Once the pre-fabricated pieces were assembled, an elaborate fantasy of dolphins, storks, lilies and bullrushes rose a majestic six metres, spraying mists into the air from all three tiers.

With the fountain installed at the confluence of paths leading from the Gardens' entrance and branching towards the river, the Christchurch Beautifying Association felt they had paid a fitting tribute to the conditions laid out in Peacock's legacy.

However, debate raged in the newspapers of the day. It was denigrated as a folly of epic proportions by some leaders of the arts community and lauded by others as a fine piece of design.

Four years later the Peacock Fountain was moved to the southeast corner of the Archery Lawn and in 1931 it was relocated again to a site west of the Archery Lawn.

Having been a highlight of the Gardens for decades, in 1949 corroded internal parts and ongoing maintenance issues forced the fascinating display to be dismantled and placed in storage.

In the second half of the 20th century, various groups endeavoured to resurrect the fountain, and finally in the early 1990s a working group was formally established and a conservation plan prepared.

Christchurch's first female mayor, Vicki Buck and councillor Margaret Murray, were pivotal in supporting the restoration and it was officially re-commissioned in 1996.

Public and Council funding provided the $270,000 required for refurbishment including the recasting of 158 of its 309 iron pieces.

Once again, the colour scheme re-ignited public debate and today the Peacock Fountain continues to entertain hundreds of thousands of locals and tourists with its outrageous flamboyance.

ABOVE: Truly original – the Peacock fountain continues to polarise public opinion of art, form and beauty with its elaborate fantasy of fish, storks, lilies and bullrushes.

BELOW: The Peacock Fountain in the early 1900s. © Christchurch City Libraries

A marvellous folly

William Sefton Moorhouse
a man who made his mark

Victorian sculptor George Anderson Lawson had notable commissions, including the Duke of Wellington monument in Liverpool and the memorial of Robert Burns in Ayr.

In 1885 he was commissioned to commemorate William Sefton Moorhouse. The bronze statue honoured the highly regarded politician most noted for his work in establishing the tunnel through the Port Hills from Lyttelton.

Moorhouse served as the second Superintendent of the Canterbury Province during the 1850s and 1860s, was repeatedly elected as a member of the New Zealand parliament and in his latter years served as the Mayor of Wellington.

ABOVE: Commemorating William Sefton Moorhouse the inscription reads, "To whose energy and perseverance Canterbury owes the tunnel between the Port Hills and the Plains."

William Sefton Moorhouse, born 1825, died 1881. Superintendent of the Canterbury Province from 1858-62 and 1866-68.

The Curator's House

Visitors entering the Botanic Gardens at the Rolleston Avenue entrance, not far from the famous Antigua Boat Sheds, are always impressed by the two-storey building that stands majestically to the left. This is the Curator's House, built in 1920 to replace the earlier, more modest single-storey cottage built in the early 1870s. Designed by Collins and Harman, the building is a combination of the Arts and Crafts tradition known as Old English or Tudor style.

The first occupants of the original house were horticulturist John Armstrong, the second curator of the Gardens, and his son Joseph. Most subsequent curators lived in the house, the last of these being the family of Alan Jolliffe in 1982 – his successor, Warwick Scadden, chose not to live there and the house was rented out until the lease expired two decades later. In 1998, the building and its garden were advertised for lease.

Meanwhile, Javier Garcia Perea and his wife Jackie Garcia Knight had been searching for a suitable site for a café. The charm of the Curator's House proved irresistible. With only a weekend to put together a submission for tenancy, they triumphed over stiff competition and opened the Curator's House Restaurant. In a superb setting among trees, lawns and flowering plants, and with the Avon River bubbling gently nearby, the restaurant serves lunch, dinner and coffee in elegant surroundings.

A condition of the tenancy was to undertake earthquake strengthening of the building. This was to prove extremely fortuitous, as the Curator's House withstood the 2010 earthquake well. The February 2011 forced its closure, although it was able to reopen in October 2012 following repairs and strengthening work.

Being a Group 3 heritage building and Category II listed by New Zealand Historic Places Trust, the Curator's House repairs were sensitively handled. They included the use of retrieved laths and a traditional plaster finish where original plaster had to be stripped off. The original stone cladding was tied into the reconstructed chimneys, while only a third of the original internal masonry was removed.

BELOW: Walkway and Gardener's Cottage, February 1910. © Canterbury Museum

Vegetable & Herb Garden

The name potager comes from the French term for kitchen garden. Typically potagers are gardens with formal, structured designs, often with raised beds, overflowing with an otherwise possibly frowned on mix of flowers, fruit, vegetables and herbs. They were popular in the 1920s when this Curator's House was built. The House is now home to a restaurant and the nearby potager is put to good use, with chefs nipping into the garden to select fresh fruit, herbs, and vegetables. This charming garden incorporates an "informal orchard" with named varieties of pears, apples, apricots, peaches and feijoas, many grown on dwarfing rootstocks. Pears are espaliered around the archways, apples fan the fences, and peaches, trimmed to manageable umbrella shapes, stand guard among the tomatoes and garlic. Vegetables abound; borage and Californian poppies, which attract insects to the gardens, proliferate, bringing a splash of colour to the beds, as do nasturtium and calendula, which help repel aphids, and also grace the restaurant meals as garnish. This working garden is managed mainly by Botanic Gardens staff. It is open to the public, who can wander the paths, be inspired by the bounty, and learn about techniques for productive gardening in small spaces.

❶ Cutleaf beech

Fagus sylvatica 'Laciniata'

Glowing golden in autumn, the cutleaf European beech with its delicate feathery leaves, that look as though they've been trimmed with pinking shears, makes a marvellous sight as it prepares to shed its leaves for winter. This tree is one of the Gardens' many treasures. It is not only an impressively large specimen, it is also fairly rare, and is on the register of New Zealand's notable trees.

The Archery Lawn

One of the most inviting locales of the Gardens, the pristine Archery Lawn is bounded by majestic trees which provide shelter and a rich tapestry of texture. Welcoming crowds for summer events this verdant expanse of lawn is prized for its contrast of floral display, water feature, sculpture and towering trees.

CLUSTER PINE

❷ Cluster pine

Pinus pinaster

Towering over even the tallest
trees in the Botanic Gardens is a
group of cluster pines.

These lofty pines encircle the main point of elevation in the Gardens,
giving it the name, the Pine Mound. Impressively tall, they sway gently
in the wind and are occasionally groomed by brave arborists, who are
admired for their ability to scale great heights. They bear huge cones,
and are beloved by the native wood pigeons (kereru) that inhabit the
Gardens. Cluster pines were used in the south of France to reclaim
sand dunes – hence their common name maritime pine – and the pines
in the Botanic Gardens fulfil the same function. The Pine Mound is one
of three original sand dunes that existed when the Botanic Gardens
were created and is the only one remaining.

The Archery Lawn

In the 1880s this lawn was used by a local archery club, which gave the impressive space its name. The moniker is now rather anachronistic, as the use of bows and arrows are banned for safety precautions (to the surprise of the occasional visitor who comes expecting to practise archery) and the only sports played here these days are the occasional game of Frisbee.

Bounded by a wall of foliage created by some of the Gardens' most notable trees, it is a very sheltered area and, being not quite rectangular, has a relaxed and interesting ambience. It's a feeling that seems to affect visitors and locals alike: most people who wander across the lush grass amble slowly to admire the giant redwoods, the pond with its interactive sculpture, or sit awhile and sunbathe.

Like much of the Gardens, it changes with the seasons, producing a range of ever-changing vistas. In winter the wide open spaces are often coated with heavy frosts that glisten and sparkle as the early morning sunshine peeks through the trees.

On autumn mornings it can be quite mysterious and atmospheric, especially when cloaked with a misty drift of fog that parts to reveal glimpses of the Temperate Asian Collection. In summer the colourful highlight is the copper beech that glows deep red amongst the green. Summer is also the season of Lazy Sundays, when the Archery Lawn hosts free concerts on Sunday afternoons. Gigs range from classical to jazz to country, and flocks of people wander in to relax, enjoy the music and mellow out on this verdant and sheltered lawn.

RIGHT: Band concert on Archery Grounds, October 1910.
© Canterbury Times photograph, Bishop Collection, Canterbury Museum

" We arrived in New Zealand 34 years ago knowing no one. Our trip to Christchurch Botanic Gardens had so many trees and plants common to Botanic Gardens in Edinburgh that we felt we were not far from home. It is a place I visit whenever I feel blue – the trees and plants, the river and birds, cheer me up no end. Lately a visit to the Gardens helps with all the earthquake woes. It has marvellous healing properties. Thank you. "

AMAMA THORNLEY

Lauded as the 'best way to unwind over summer', the Lazy Sundays series of free musical performances is a favourite on the city's events calendar. Attracting around 2000 music fans every Sunday during the height of summer it features a range of talented artists. Guests pack a picnic and a blanket and relax for an afternoon in the laid-back atmosphere of the Archery Lawn.

❸ Monkey puzzle

Araucaria araucana

With its branches flicking gently upwards like a carefully coiffured hairstyle and its naked trunk, this monkey puzzle tree looks rather like a giant lollipop on a pockmarked stalk. These marks are from the branches that fall off when the plant is a juvenile – a long time ago for this tree, planted in 1870. A cousin of the kauri, the monkey puzzle is native to Chile and Argentina and is sometimes known as the Chilean pine. It was discovered by botanists in about 1780 and introduced to England about a decade later by English naturalist Archibald Menzies. This gentleman, when dining with the Governor of Chile, slipped a few of the nuts that were served for dessert into his pocket. Did he know what he was pocketing? Probably! He planted these on board ship and arrived back in England with five tiny *Araucaria* trees, one of which existed in Kew Gardens until 1892.

Regret
by Sam Mahon

A haunting carousel of bronze masks linked to a spidery ten-metre high steel tower, showers eerie reflections onto a leaf-strewn pond in the Archery Lawn.

Viewers are encouraged to participate in engineering the fountain by way of a hand lever activating the ingenious ensemble of steel and bronze.

A blindfolded figure rises to reach out across the pond in a pose reminiscent of a player in the childhood game of Blind Man's Bluff.

Painter, sculptor, writer and conservationist, Sam Mahon's ingenious work titled 'Regret' was created in response to the kinetic theme of wind and water for the third Sculpture in the Gardens show November 1997 - April 1998.

It is said the work was made with the intention of reflecting the "messy reality of human life".

Enthralling visitors of all ages, the sculptor suggested 'Regret' could remain in the Gardens if a sponsor was found. Fortunately, adventure race innovator and art patron Robin Judkins offered his support.

ABOVE: The bronze masks of 'Regret'.

© Liz Clark

Iris Border

"[It] strikes the eye from afar. The Irises are a beautiful study full of air and life."

So wrote Theo van Gogh to his brother Vincent, in response to his famous painting. Indeed there is something magical and ethereal about these delicate blooms, which provide a glorious burst of colour in the Botanic Gardens' dedicated Iris Border.

KAURI

4 Kauri

Agathis australis

Arguably one of New Zealanders' favourite trees, the kauri is also one of those ancient plants that has survived from the Jurassic era and is related to the similarly ancient monkey puzzle tree and wollemi pine. Although kauri forests are specific to the warmer climes in the north of the North Island, kauri also flourish in the Botanic Gardens. This tall outstanding specimen on the Archery Lawn was planted in 1920 by Edward, Prince of Wales. Recently several smaller trees from the Western Lawn of the New Zealand Garden were moved to the new Gondwana Garden, which will feature the direct descendants of plants and trees from prehistoric times.

The Archery Lawn | 49

CORK OAK.

⑤ Cork oak
Quercus suber

The intriguingly nubbly bark of the cork oak (*Quercus suber*) is the source of the cork we would find in our wine bottles, as cork tiles and sometimes in fashion trims. A close look and it's easy to see it is indeed like the cork that keeps the bubbles in our French champagne. The tree is an evergreen from Southern Europe and North Africa, and in these countries the bark from commercial cork trees is harvested every eight to 10 years for the wine industry. Care is taken not to damage the living tissue below, and the bark gradually regenerates. This tree has not been harvested.

To enter the avenue of majestic linden trees in mid-summer and watch the dappled sunshine filter through the archway of lime-coloured leaves and dainty white flowers, petals drifting ground-ward is to be transported from the Antipodes directly to Europe.

❻ Lime or linden tree

Tilea x europaea

Unter den Linden. The Botanic Gardens have their own lime avenue, which forms Beswick's Walk. It's not as grand or famous as that avenue in Berlin, but is beautiful nevertheless. The trees were planted in 1917 and the avenue is named for Henry Joseph Beswick, a longstanding Chairman of the Christchurch Domains Board.

LIME OR LINDEN

Herbaceous Border

A riot of colour and texture in spring, summer, and autumn, the Herbaceous Border hibernates in winter.

Traditionally, an herbaceous border was symbolic of the English country garden, where collections of herbaceous perennials grouped closely together created a dramatic effect through sheer size. This border, which is over 100 metres long, was once thought to be the longest in a public garden in New Zealand. It was designed in traditional fashion during the late 1920s and rejuvenated in the early 2000s to designs based on modern English herbaceous borders. European and American (Prairie School) influences have been introduced. Grasses and succulents have joined the traditional perennial parade of salvias, monardas, asters, pulmonarias, geraniums, cannas, phlox, red hot pokers, euphorbias, dahlias and others, adding variety in form, colour and texture.

One of the beauties of the herbaceous border is that it is ever changing, and every month reveals a different combination. In autumn the border has its final fling with seed heads adding interest and an autumn cutback gives late bloomers like cannas, dahlias, and chrysanthemums their day in the limelight. It also reveals plants that are already starting to green up for their spring display. So while the "lucky last" salvias will probably depart with the first hard frost in May, by August or September we can expect the early flowering pulmonarias to lift their delicate heads and lead the way for next season's herbaceous delights.

ABOVE: Atop a stone cairn sits the bronze Hunter Sundial edged with engravings on four brass plaques of the biblical passage from Isaiah 35:1. "The desert shall rejoice, and blossom as the rose".

❼ Redwoods
Sequoiadendron giganteum

There are six massive redwoods along the edge of the Archery Lawn, and one, bigger than the rest, is a favourite with adventurous kids. They swing on the long, loopy branches that reach to the ground and play hide and seek on the carpets of dropped needles. They attract grownups too, some choosing to use the solid trunks as a back rest while they read in the sun, their enormous size affording privacy and personal space. Redwoods can grow up to 90 metres high and their bark can be up to half a metre thick, a feature thought to save them from raging bushfires in their native California. These trees were raised from seed from California and planted in 1873.

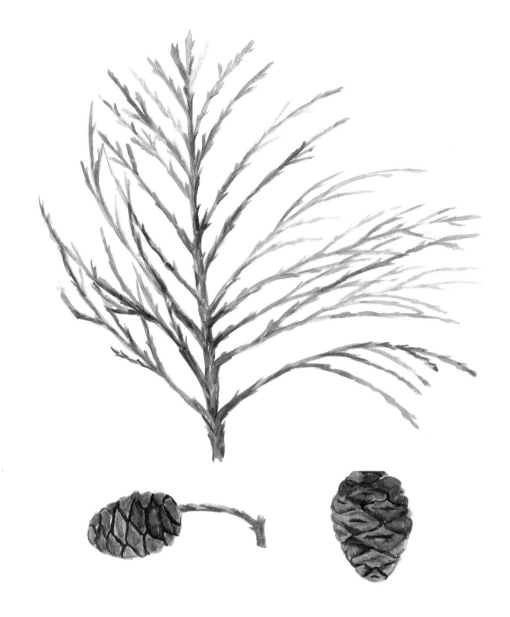

" The Botanic Gardens is a place to visit again and again. I have memories of my children running around azalea beds in spring, kicking golden leaves under giant trees in autumn, swinging on trees, climbing in the playground, canoeing on the Avon in summer, feeding ducks, ducklings and trout. I have taken friends to admire rhododendrons. I have drawn inspiration for our developing home garden. I have spent many hours observing and drawing giant trees and the many water features. It is my haven in the city.   HAWWA MOORE. "

It's no wonder that one of the redwoods in the Gardens is known as "The Swing Tree."

Maple Border

The beautiful, delicate Maple Border, which forms a lacy canopy when in full leaf, should really be called the Japanese Maple Border as it is home to only the Japanese variety of these trees.

Although gnarly old trunks give the impression that the trees are really old, they were probably planted in the 1930s and it is possible that many of the cultivars were donated by Nairn's, a local nursery. Early photos, taken when the trees were small, show that they were underplanted with bedding plants like tulips and pansies which thrived in the sun. Nowadays, the border forms a sheltering canopy for shade loving hydrangeas and hellebores.

The *Woodlands*

From the Southern entrance, shady parades of towering trees march riverside welcoming visitors through all seasons.

Narcissi wave a springtime joy to honour Wordsworth's pen, dappled light sparkles on summer waters, and burnished leaves fall until winter strips branches bare revealing deciduous lines.

Poignantly, it was the first New Zealand-born curator, James McPherson, who identified the stunning potential for a daffodil collection beneath the woodland trees.

The people of Canterbury gifted more than 16,000 bulbs to start the revelry of golden blossoms now attracting hundreds of thousands of visitors every year.

TAKING FLIGHT

Taking Flight
by Phil Price

An intriguing form arises from amid woodland trees – elegant bronze wings alight from an oval bed of concrete to form an early piece designed by renowned Christchurch sculptor Phil Price.

Disguising pipes drawing sweet artesian waters for visitors to sip, this striking drinking fountain was commissioned and gifted by the Canterbury Branch of the Institute of Foundrymen to the city in 1993.

Taking Flight was cast at the Woolston Foundry and was funded with support from local businesses.

> My memory is, as a student of Horticulture in the 1960s, visiting the Botanic Gardens to learn the names of the plants from the labels and trying to memorise them, then finding out that the signwriter also produced wonderful botanical prints of many of the plants.
>
> MICHAEL

Acclimatisation Societies

The actual site of the original hatchery where the first brown trout arrived in New Zealand. They were reared in September 1867 by the North Canterbury Acclimatisation Society.

Acclimatisation garden, Hagley Park, February 1905.
© Charles Beken photograph, Canterbury Museum

The introduction of flora and fauna from other parts of the world was widely believed by 19th century botanical and zoological enthusiasts to enhance a region and support natural history and scientific study.

Isidore Geoffroy Saint-Hilaire initiated the original acclimatisation organisation - La Societé Zoologique d'Acclimatation – in Paris in 1854.

With a desire to re-create their homelands and develop economic potential from agricultural and horticultural pursuit, early pioneers, particularly in the American and Oceanic colonies, rapidly followed the French in establishing their own acclimatisation societies.

The North Canterbury Acclimatisation Society was founded in 1864 and with an allocation of lands within Hagley Park, began introducing foreign trees, plants, birds, fish and animals.

Once known as "the zoo" the gardens also played host to exotic species including bears and monkeys, as well as Australian imports of emus and kangaroos.

SCULPTURE

The Wrestlers
by Llew Summers

A sculpture rejoicing in the human form elicited outrage when it was first installed beside the banks of the Avon in 1990.

Christchurch artist Llew Summers' voluptuous entanglement of naked bodies was not considered an appropriate artwork to grace a public space until it was titled 'The Wrestlers'.

Much of Summers' work celebrates the beauty of the nude human form and this piece invites wonder at the power and flexibility of bodies at sport and play.

Cast in terrazzo – a composite of marble chip and cement – 'The Wrestlers' joins a collection of Summers' works in public and private spaces throughout New Zealand.

> During 1990, an untitled piece of sculpture by Llew Summers was sited in the woodland, close to the Avon River. Several complaints were received from parents who believed it appeared to represent a couple in the throes of passion, and found it embarrassing when questioned by their children. All was resolved when the sculptor was asked to give the piece a title – his response was 'The Wrestlers'. From the day when the inscription was attached, no further complaints were received.
>
> WARWICK SCADDEN. CURATOR 1983-1999

Heritage Rose Garden

Rosa banksiae 'Alba Plena'

Rosa 'Penelope'

Rosa 'Zephirine Drouhin'

Bandsmen's Memorial Rotunda

This is an early memorial in New Zealand dedicated to those bandsmen who lost their lives during World War I.

Set in Harman's Grove beneath stately trees including ash, oak and sycamore, the Bandsmen's Memorial Rotunda was officially opened on 19 September 1926, by Sir Heaton Rhodes. It was built as a dedication to the Canterbury bandsmen killed in World War I. Designed by architects S & A Luttrell, the rotunda overlooks the Primula Garden, making it especially attractive in spring.

Over the years the rotunda has been a popular venue for a wide range of musical entertainment – brass bands, pipe bands and string quartets.

Harman's Grove

This two hectare section of the Gardens is named after a member of the early Christchurch Domains Board. It's everything a grove should be and more, as it is rather larger than you'd expect a small group of trees to be. It has many fine specimens of European trees such as oak, ash, and hornbeam – stately individuals – much admired for their cool shade in summer and their attractive autumn colours. It is home to an interesting, semi-circular stone seat with two of the stones engraved with the initials FCM and DRM.

BELOW: Lady and child walking past Riccarton Avenue Gates which are near the Bandsmen's Memorial Rotunda, 1930s. © Christchurch Botanic Gardens

The Central Gardens
& Conservatories

Arches laden with summer blooms beckon wanderers on the central lawns. Stepping through the bowers is to be welcomed by a profusion of colour and the romantic airs of the Rose Garden.

In a resplendent display, more than 100 beds hosting a flourishing collection of hybrid floribunda, climbers, miniatures and standard roses encircle a sundial centerpiece.

The World Peace Bell

A bicycle ride for peace...

Christchurch's World Peace Bell

Thanks to an heroic 3777 kilometre cycle journey over 71 days by New Zealand author and photographer Roy Sinclair and his partner Haruko Morita, Christchurch has the privilege of hosting New Zealand's World Peace Bell.

Roy was fascinated by the story of Japanese peace advocate Chiyoji Nakagawa [1905-1972], Mayor of Uwajima in Shikoku during 1959-1967 and 1971-1972.

In 1950, Nakagawa initiated a new bell to replace the one seized by military from the Taihei Temple during World War II. "The Bell of Banzai for Absolute Peace" was cast with the inclusion of coins from 26 countries.

Nakagawa was invited to Paris for the sixth UN General Assembly in 1951 and there he coordinated the donation of coins from 65 participating countries as well as nine gold coins donated by Pope Pius XII created from statues of Christ and the virgin Mary.

Mirroring the design of the Taihei Temple bell, Nakagawa cast a new bell incorporating the coins. In 1954 it was presented as a symbol of peace to the United Nations in New York and rests on soils from Hiroshima and Nagasaki.

It was Chiyoji Nakagawa's hope that no nation should ever again experience an atomic bomb attack.

A decade after Mayor Nakagawa died, the World Peace Bell Association was formed to continue his dream. The first replica bell was placed in the Peace Park at Soya Misaki, on the northernmost tip of Hokkaido.

In January 2001, Roy and Haruko travelled by small motor train to visit the site at Soya. The wintry seascapes and intensely cold temperatures (minus 22 degrees) inspired Roy to write a newspaper story 'Slow Tracks to Wakkanai.'

This story attracted the attention of the World Peace Bell Association in Tokyo and Roy declared he would ride his bicycle the length of Japan if the group would agree to gift a World Peace Bell to New Zealand.

In August 2004 the couple returned to Soya in order to commence the challenging ride. The world peace bell for New Zealand was cast like the original with coins from UN member nations.

Funds were raised to help with transportation and the pavilion housing for the bell. Ngāi Tahu donated a pounamu carving, which was placed with a piece of black granite into the reflection pond beneath the bell.

On 3 October 2006, the Mayor of Christchurch Garry Moore and World Peace Bell Association Tokyo representative Keizo Ohashi raised the sound of the bell's first gong in its Botanic Garden setting.

Every year in 20 places across the globe, the peace bells are rung to celebrate World Peace Day.

⑧ Albert Edward oak
Quercus robur

One of many oaks in the Gardens, this common oak known as the Albert Edward oak was planted on 9 July 1863 to commemorate the marriage of Queen Victoria's son Albert Edward, Prince of Wales and Her Royal Highness Alexandra of Denmark. Its planting date is considered to be the commencement date of the Gardens.

ALBERT EDWARD OAK

Heather Garden

This friendly little garden of low growing shrubs in raised beds is at its colourful best in autumn, winter, and spring, although it does put on a show throughout the year.

It consists of a collection of two closely related genera *Calluna* (heaths) and *Erica* (heathers). This is an important garden, as you can no longer buy heaths (apart from those with double flowers which are infertile) as they are classed as noxious plants. Because they are not necessarily long-lived, the curator of the garden is concentrating on propagating the existing cultivars to preserve the collection. Heathers were very popular in the 1960s when this garden was redeveloped in 1967. After drifting out of fashion, these acid loving plants are again creating interest amongst home gardeners, perhaps because they are comparatively easy care and put on great shows of winter colour.

To display this collection at its best and create extra interest in summer, seven deciduous *Stewartia pseudocamellia*, which have colourful bark in winter and beautiful single white flowers in summer, have recently been planted on the edge of the Heather Garden.

The Rock Garden

With its large stone, hillocks and meandering pathways, the Rock Garden is a 'mini garden' beloved of children. First planted in the 1930s, it was extended in the 1960s, when stone paths were the height of garden fashion. Mostly home to bulbs, ericas and other rock plants, it has a climate that is more extreme than other areas of the garden; very cold in winter and warm and sheltered in spring and summer. In spring, when the magenta azaleas are in full bloom, they are reflected in the lily pond. Truly a sight to behold.

" The funny thing was, I let out a gasp, and Nikki got a fright. She looked at my face and thought something really terrible had happened. It was just such a surprise to see the Himalayan blue poppies (*Meconopsis grandis*) blooming. They were looking gorgeous, glowing blue in the shade. A favourite of mine, they are one of the few truly blue flowers in existence. "

CELIA PRUDEN RECALLS WALKING IN THE ROCK GARDEN OCTOBER 2011 WITH HER MOTHER PENNY AND SISTER NICOLA.

The Dahlia Garden

These beds, a more recent addition to the Gardens, surround the
Rose Garden and are greatly admired by overseas visitors, when
the plants are in full bloom. They are the perfect showcase for New
Zealand bred cultivars, which form a large part of the collection.

"The dahlia you brought to our isle
Your praises for ever shall speak;
Mid gardens as sweet as your smile,
And in colour as bright as your cheek." – Lord Holland

WESTFELTON YEW

❾ Westfelton yew

Taxus baccata 'Dovastoniana'

This tree is quite spectacular. Its long pendulous branchlets reach to the ground, creating a private tent. It is rumoured to be the place where schoolboys would sneak for a forbidden cigarette. Even now, it receives judicious trimming to ensure it doesn't provide cover for other nefarious deeds. Gorgeous to look at, all parts of the yew are extremely poisonous to humans and animals, except for the aril, which is the fleshy red part surrounding the seed. This handsome tree is considered to be the best of two known specimens of this variety in New Zealand. The history of the tree is not known, but it was believed to have been over 100 years old in 1984.

⑩ Atlas cedar

Cedrus atlantica

An elegant tree, the Atlas cedar has the most exquisite female cones. Neat and tidy, they are almost smooth whorls that look like handcrafted Christmas decorations, wound in careful circles. They show this dainty craftsmanship off, sitting perkily pointing upwards on needle-like leaves on the tree's lush branches. A member of the Pinaceae family, they are native to the Atlas Mountains of northwest Africa.

ATLAS CEDAR

The Rose Garden

Visitors from near and far flock to the Rose Garden during the months of November to March when it is in full bloom, as it is truly a breathtaking sight.

Its formal circular design, pergolas and archways are covered with climbers, and it is encircled by a protective yew hedging that cleverly displays the colourful blooms to their best advantage. The sheltered site and Christchurch's temperate climate, plus the careful stewardship of the Gardens' rosarian staff ensure that the hundreds of rose plants in the garden retain optimum health. The original Rose Garden was established in 1909 and was considered the largest and finest in Australasia. Rectangular in shape, the design was based on the rose garden owned by the Duchess of Sutherland in Herefordshire, England. It was redeveloped in the 1930s in the circular design. In the 1950s the mirror pool at the centre was replaced by a large memorial sundial.

The garden contains cultivars and hybrids of modern garden roses including bush, climbing, standard and miniature roses. Outside the yew hedging and almost appearing to be holding hands, are recently planted espaliered heritage apple trees. They add intrigue and interest in this colourful area.

PERFECT MOMENT

Rose Sculpture
by Raymond Herber

Commissioned to craft seasonal emblems, North Canterbury metal artist Raymond Herber used the forge and anvil to encourage these monumental symbols to emerge from his steel.

A sundial dedicated to the memory of Thomas Stevenson replaced the mirror pool as the central feature of the rose garden in 1954.

THE ROSE GARDEN SUNDIAL

LEFT: Rising from a double layer of octagonal granite steps, the tapered stone cairn supports a black marble disc.

BELOW: The bronze shadow marker and engravings to mark compass, clock and calendar points are accompanied by a circlet of flowers.

I have a bemused memory from the early 1960s of being propositioned in the rose garden on a beautiful sunny day. There were lots of people around so I couldn't believe what was happening. The opening line being, 'Have you ever considered being a model? I would like to take some photographs of you.' No I hadn't, and I didn't have any photographs taken. I was 19 years old and very innocent at the time.

⓫ Purple beech
Fagus sylvatica var. purpurea

This purple beech, situated south of the Rose Garden, is an impressive and breathtakingly beautiful tree. Rich purple-black, plum coloured leaves change to burnished gold in autumn. This deciduous tree, which is native to Europe, is one of many purple beech's in the Gardens. One on the Armstrong Lawn was planted by Lord Jellicoe in 1919.

⑫ Alpine ash
Eucalyptus delegatensis

A twisted trunk like a ceremonial turban and, high above, smooth branches draped with undulating ribbons of bark. The alpine ash (*Eucalyptus delegatensis*) is a mountain species from Australia. With its enormous girth and great height, it is the largest tree in the Gardens and the largest of its species in New Zealand.

Even visitors to the Gardens from its native country are amazed by its size. In its native environment these eucalypts, like many other Australian trees, are consumed by bush fires before they grow this big. This is nature's way of propagating, as extreme heat opens the capsules and the seeds inside are dispersed.

With its enormous girth and great height, it is the largest tree in the Gardens and the largest of its species in New Zealand.

The Fragrant Garden

Nestled comfortably on the southwest aspect of the conservatories this area of the Gardens gets good protection from prevailing winds. It was established in 1990 as a sesquicentennial year project with significant financial support from Canterbury women's organisations. As a garden developed around the sense of smell, it is a special place for those with impaired vision. The layout recognises this and a series of wide paths, raised planters and structures for climbers offer safe, easy access while providing excellent conditions for a wide range of fragrant trees, shrubs, perennials, annuals and bulbs.

Edgeworthia chrysantha

Hyacinthus orientalis

Cuningham House

Known for its collection of luxuriant tropical plants, Cuningham House is an impressive and stately structure and is listed with the New Zealand Historic Places Trust.

Cuningham House was opened in 1923, the result of a bequest by Mr C A C Cuningham, who was a great admirer of the Botanic Gardens. The building boasts sweeping staircases that lead to a peripheral gallery.

An extensive collection of tropical plants is displayed upstairs, although both levels of Cuningham House share collections that include anthuriums and dracaenas, dieffenbachias, hoyas and peperomias.

While visitors have long admired its delicate orchids and spiky bromeliads, Cuningham House is also home to colourful bougainvilleas and poinsettias, as well as larger specimen palms, a nikau and a few screw pines. The pitcher plant and strangely named fruit salad plant (*Monstera deliciosa*) have fascinated generations of visitors.

Shade-loving plants have been kept downstairs: the tree canopy created by the taller plants blocks out much of the light, thereby allowing the ground floor area to accommodate plant groups that require low light conditions.

ABOVE: Cuningham House with a section of the glorious Rose Garden. © Christchurch Botanic Gardens

ABOVE: Several marble sculptures gifted to the Gardens adorn the conservatories. One cheekily depicts carousing cherub-like putti.

© Peter Morath

Townend House

Townend House was named after Annie Quayle Townend, who immigrated to New Zealand from England in the mid-1860s. Daughter of George Henry Moore, the richest of the 19th century South Island run-holders, she lived most of her adult life with her father at Glenmark Station, Waipara, where a lavish house and magnificent garden were established. Upon her father's death, she is said to have become the wealthiest heiress in the country.

Annie Quayle Moore married Joseph Henry Townend when she was in her fifties. The couple had no children. She died in 1914, her estate making possible the purchase of the original Townend House from Allan Mclean's 'Holly Lea' and transfer to the Botanic Gardens. The old wooden structure was demolished in 1954-55 and replaced by the present Townend House. This new building was constructed over the footprint of its predecessor and measures over 19 metres by 9, giving it its rectangular shape. The second largest of the six conservatories at the Botanic Gardens, it is connected to Cuningham House by a covered passageway.

Temperature and ventilation are carefully controlled to ensure optimum conditions for the bright and cheerful greenhouse plants housed here.

Careful planning on the part of Botanic Gardens staff has 25 to 30 different collections of flowering plants displayed in glorious colour at Townend House annually. These include begonias and cyclamen, pelargoniums, primula, purple bells, sage and schizanthus.

Garrick House

The conservatory housing an impressive collection of cacti and succulents from around the world was completed in 1957. It was given the name Garrick House in honour of Mr M Garrick, who had previously donated a large number of these plants to the Gardens, but is often referred to as the Cactus House.

Garrick House was created to give visitors the impression that they are standing in a desert. Red volcanic rock and soil were brought across from Banks Peninsula when the conservatory was being built, in accordance with the desert theme, and a fine diorama depicting desert landscapes from Africa to the Americas forms a striking backdrop to the display.

On show are exhibits from North and South America, as well as Africa. Many are grown in pots.

The collection is one of the largest public displays of cacti in New Zealand. The mainly American cacti on display here include the alpine *Tephrocactus*, *Opuntia*, *Oreocereus*, *Notocactus*, *Cereus*, *Cleistocactus*, *Echinocereus*, *Ferocactus*, and *Mammillaria*.

Cacti come not only from hot dry desert areas. There are species that may be covered with snow for a large part of the year, as well as others found growing in tropical rainforests or beach sands.

Orchid Genus *Vanola*

Gilpin House

To get to the modest sized Gilpin House, visitors must first pass through Townend House and the adjacent Garrick House.

Built in the 1960s, Gilpin House is kept at a temperature of around 19° Celsius, and at a high level of humidity. This environment well suits the varieties of plants held there: tropical orchids, bromeliads, tillandsias and the curious carnivorous plants. The display is changed regularly so as to better exhibit plants of interest as they flower.

The conservatory is named after Huia Gilpin, who became assistant director (curator) of the Botanic Gardens in 1949 and director in 1955. Gilpin was also responsible for the building of Garrick House and the reconstruction of Townend House, and was in office when the Botanic Gardens celebrated its centenary in 1963. He remained as curator until 1979.

Gilpin and his wife Florence took an interest in the apprentices who studied plant identification and organised seed collection field trips. The apprentices were invited to visit them at the Curator's House, where books on gardening and horticulture lined the bookshelves.

Heliamphora minor

Huia Gilpin has the distinction of being the first person in New Zealand to pass the National Diploma in Horticulture by examination in 1939. He went on to study landscape architecture at the Canterbury College of Art.

Strelitzia reginae

13 Monterey cypress
Cupressus macrocarpa

This is quite possibly the most photographed tree in the Gardens! Not because it is a great beauty, or because of its great size, but because it must be the most climbed up and sat upon by children, of course providing their adoring parents and grandparents the perfect photo opportunity. Several children at a time can fit in the great rift between the lowest branches, and the trunk is worn smooth by tiny bottoms. To one local family it is 'the measuring tree' as four generations have made the trek to the Gardens to be measured against the trunk of this venerable stalwart. Known to most Kiwis simply as the macrocarpa, it is also called the Monterey cypress, and is endemic to the Central Coast of California.

MONTEREY CYPRESS

Foweraker House

The smallest of the Botanic Gardens conservatories is an alpine house. First opened in 1967, the house was renamed Foweraker House in 1981 for alpine plant enthusiast Jean Foweraker who donated many alpine plants to the Gardens.

With its cool environment, this standalone conservatory is the ideal location for the display of indigenous and exotic alpine plants.

Dwarf conifers and saxifrages form the backdrop to an extensive and ever-changing display of flowering plants – spring heralds *Fritillaria*, *Narcissus* and *Tulipa*, followed by *Helichrysum* and *Celmisia* in summer, and specimens such as *Oxalis*, *Cyclamen* and *Narcissus* in autumn.

The collection is potted to protect the plants from the elements. This allows the plants to grow in their own specialised soil conditions while avoiding overhead watering. Many of the plants are small in size and are therefore not suitable for planting out in the Rock Garden.

TOP RIGHT: *Edmondia pinifolia*
MIDDLE: *Helichrysum coralloides*
BOTTOM: *Aciphylla aurea*

The Fern House

As suggested by its name,
the Fern House is home to a remarkable
display of New Zealand ferns.

Located to the north of the conservatories at the Botanic Gardens, the Fern House stands proudly on its own.

A small stream meanders through the house, lulling visitors with the tinkling sound of running water. A narrow path follows the stream as it winds around the display, allowing visitors to see all parts as they wander through.

Ponga or tree ferns are prominent, in particular the New Zealand icon the silver fern (*Cyathea dealbata*).

Ponga logs clad the inside walls of the house and provide a home to several species of epiphytic ferns, while the tree ferns offer shelter for the more delicate species that grow below them.

Fern House was built in 1955 following bequests from James Foster and Mary Rothney Orr.

The climate within the Fern House, which houses some beautifully delicate ferns, enables the cultivation of a number of New Zealand ferns that would otherwise be difficult to grow outdoors in Christchurch.

Mosses, liverworts and several species of indigenous orchids also thrive in the damp shady bush that the Fern House provides.

Peeking from amid the luscious fronds of pongas in the Fern House is a trio of giant moa. These genius works are the creations of Manchester sculptor Jack Marsden-Mayer.

Moa in the Fern House
by Jack Marsden-Mayer

Constructed from hundreds of driftwood segments and galvanized roofing screws, the largest tribute to the extinct bird species stands nearly three metres high.

Originally commissioned for Auckland landscapers Adam Shuter and Tony Murrell's 2013 Ellerslie Garden Show entry – 'Modern Day Moa' – the sculptures wowed crowds and the council was encouraged to purchase the artworks.

In a striking coincidence, the English city of Bristol will also host two gigantic moa. Woven from willow, these colossal works are being crafted by artist Sally Meadows, to stand among the New Zealand native collection in the University of Bristol Botanic Gardens late 2013.

14 Maidenhair tree
Ginkgo biloba

Even though they are living fossils they make a charming couple, the male and female ginkgos. The female tree with its tall and elegant structure and growth habit and dainty feathery leaves gives the tree its common name of maidenhair and is the most striking. But in autumn, beware! While the cooler weather brings beautiful golden foliage to both trees, the female then bears fruit that is particularly malodorous. They are prized by people from Asia (the tree is native to China) who arrive, equipped with gloves, to collect the fruits which have tasty nuts hidden inside. This pair of ginkgos were planted on Arbor Day in 1936 by garden staff and were originally intended to be the start of a ginkgo avenue.

15 Dawn redwood
Metasequoia glyptostroboides

Another fossil tree, the deciduous dawn redwood was thought to be extinct until discovered by a forester in Sichuan, Central China in 1941. It is still critically endangered. In 1948, the Arnold Arboretum of Harvard University sent an expedition to collect seeds and, soon after, seedling trees were distributed free to various universities and arboreta worldwide for growth trials. This tree is not one of those distributed globally but is believed to be the second generation of one. This precious, fast growing tree was planted in 1949.

"I have fond memories of taking our three boys to the Botanic Gardens. They loved the paddling pool, walking around the Gardens in the different seasons and ending up at the Art Gallery or Museum. When they were young scouts and cubs they went to the NZ plant section and took plaster casts of the different leaves. I still love going to the Gardens, they are a great asset to Christchurch."

NGAIRE POWER, CASHMERE GARDEN CLUB

© Priscilla Chapman

The New Zealand
& Water Gardens

Evoking a stroll within a
Monet masterpiece, the
Water Garden's serenity
seeps into the soul offering
a glimpse of a more blissful
existence and a chance to
reflect upon the simple truth
of nature's beauty.

NEW ZEALAND BEECH TREES

Cockayne Memorial Garden

Elegant towers of totara and lancewoods, interlaced with kakabeak and kowhai, manuka and hebe are the backdrop to the mounds of alpine plants and grasses forming a living tribute to famed New Zealand botanist Dr Leonard Cockayne.

Instigated by the Canterbury branch of the Royal Society of New Zealand in 1938, the Cockayne Memorial Garden honours one man's lifetime of influential botanical discoveries.

Originally from England, Cockayne began collecting and swapping seeds with other enthusiasts in 1885, at first from his small farmlet at Styx near Christchurch and subsequently from his experimental garden, Tarata, in the sandy New Brighton dunes.

He explored many of the nation's most unique botanical environs including surveys of the Chathams and Stewart Island, as well as forays even further south, into the sub-Antarctic Auckland and Campbell Islands.

Stimulating new areas of botanical research here and overseas, Cockayne promoted the observation of flora in their natural habitat and became fascinated with the science of hybridisation and plant ecology.

A prolific writer, Cockayne published hundreds of articles in local and international journals, and authored several books, the first being a collection of his commentaries, *New Zealand Plants and their Story*, in 1910.

He actively promoted conservation at government level and encouraged the development of the Department of Scientific and Industrial Research.

Cockayne held office in many national organisations, received numerous honours, awards and acknowledgements including the Royal Society of London's Darwin Medal.

The Cockayne Memorial Garden is a popular wedding venue for couples seeking a natural backdrop with a choir of New Zealand birdsong.

ABOVE: Yellow kowhai.

LEFT: Colourful hebe.

New Zealand Garden

A myriad of continual greens pierced by striking blooms form a Klimt-like collage in the New Zealand garden.

KAURI

Eden of Aotearoa.

Seeking the cool and quiet shade, tui sip from gilded trumpets of kowhai, sample kōtukutuku's purple berries and flit amid kakabeak's scarlet flares. In a massive burst of starry florets, kereru feast oblivious to their hosts' status as the earth's largest lily – tī koūka, the cabbage tree.

Watched over by the prized totara, sweetly scented beech trees seep honeydew beside bright hebes, manuka and the peppery horopito and kawakawa.

This treasured mosaic of native trees, bush, grasses, ferns, and alpine plants, nurtured by many generations of curators, botanical friends and advocates, stands serene amidst its exotic neighbours.

ABOVE: Step into a world of New Zealand native trees, bush, grasses, ferns and alpine plants and let your imagination drift to pre-European times in this gentle, serene setting.

The Water Garden

Rising from the pond's edge, gunnera spread immense leaves, dwarfing clusters of reeds and rushes, all competing for the attention so often reserved for the darlings of the pond – the water lilies. Flourishing blooms amid vibrant lime pads enchant visitors with their tranquil charms. Children crouch at the water's edge spying on dragonflies and wishing for a glimpse of the fairies that surely must alight on this storybook vista.

Te Puna Ora
The Spring of Life

Kaitiaki Kiwa by Riki Manuel
Celtic Rock Engraving by Douglas Woods

Sacred waters are a place of pilgrimage for many cultures and in 1992 the Christchurch City Council committed to celebrating the alpine-fed waters flowing beneath the Gardens with the creation of Te Puna Ora.

Flowing all year into a small pond, the sweet tasting waters of Te Puna Ora are fed from an artesian source more than 58 metres underground.

Two rock carvings were commissioned to mark this tribute to the life-giving properties of water.

'Kaitiaki Kiwa' – the embodiment of a water spirit, is the work of master carver, printmaker and moko artist Riki Manuel (Ngāti Porou) and expresses the healing energy found within pure artesian water.

A Celtic-style rock engraving by sculptor and painter Douglas Woods (Ngāi Tahu) embodies the quality of the aquifers and symbolises the elements of the cosmos and the unity of all life.

The use of a 'triskele' spiral symbol was inspired by the megalithic art forms revealed in the ancient monument at Newgrange, County Meath, in Ireland and appreciates the commonality between Māori and Celtic motifs.

The
Azalea &
Magnolia
Gardens

Magnificent blossoms of rhododendrons, horse
chestnuts, azaleas and magnolias embellish the western
garden entrance in a springtime spectacular.

16 Magnolia

Magnolia campbellii

From the formation of silky buds during winter
to its ebullient outbursts of bold blossoms on
otherwise bare branches, the magnificent *Magnolia
campbellii* near the western entrance
to the Botanic Gardens is a breathtaking sight.
This large, statuesque tree is the harbinger of
spring for hardworking Gardens staff. When the
delicate pink buds appear on the bare branches
and start to unfurl they know that the floriferous
show that heralds spring is about to begin.
M campbellii is a species from the Himalayas.
It is the largest of the magnolias and its cultivars
are amongst the earliest to flower.

Stretching out her arms so impressively, the
magnolia demands attention. Like a magician she
produces, from tightly closed buds, a profusion of
colour; unfurling her heart to all.

17 Bhutan pine

Pinus wallichiana

A Bhutan pine was planted by His Holiness the 14th Dalai Lama of Tibet on the occasion of his first visit to Christchurch on 16 May, 1992. Beside it is a 'mani stone' carved with 'Om Mani Padme Hum' a Buddhist prayer for the peace and liberation of all peoples. The tree is perfectly at home in the Pinetum, surrounded by the collection of pines and related conifers that are planted for research, education, and display.

Gondwana
& the Western End

Recreating geological links to an ancient world, the Gondwana Garden development seeks to shed light on the mystery of the origin of our Southern Hemisphere floras in a Jurassic landscape.

WOLLEMI PIINE

18 Wollemi pine
Wollemia nobilis

The Wollemi pine is a living treasure, so precious that it is protected by a cage. One of the most ancient and rarest trees in the world, this living fossil from the Jurassic age was believed to be extinct until a group of these prehistoric trees was discovered in the Blue Mountains in Australia in 1994. One of these rare plants was gifted to the late Dr David Given, former Curator at the Gardens, who was internationally renowned for his work in conserving New Zealand native plants and was a passionate Wollemi pine enthusiast. Approval was gained for the release of the plant in New Zealand, which was grown by Greg Kitson of Ambrosia Nurseries. The first Wollemi pine to be planted in New Zealand, it commemorates the 150th anniversary of the Gardens. Despite the name, it is not a pine, but is more closely related to other ancient trees, the New Zealand kauri and the Chilean monkey puzzle.

Mysterious and ancient, with plantings that hark back to the Jurassic era when New Zealand was taking shape as part of that vast southern land mass known as Gondwanaland, the Gondwana Garden is an exciting new area for the Botanic Gardens. It was launched during the Gardens' 150th anniversary year, with the planting of the rare and ancient Wollemi pine that was in existence when dinosaurs roamed the forests 200 million years ago. The garden, which will be many years in the making, will feature other ancient plants from the Jurassic period that flourished in the Southern land mass and have evolved and adapted over time. "It will look different from today's landscapes and hopefully it will feel ancient, like something we imagine from 150 million years ago," said Gardens curator Dr John Clemens. This modern Jurassic Park is located near the Children's Playground and promises to be a magical place for kids and adults alike.

The Hall Lawn

The Memorial Walk is across the Avon River opposite the Hall Lawn, named for Sir John Hall, Premier of New Zealand from 1879 to 1882, who supported votes for women and moved the Bill that gave them the franchise.

The Kate Sheppard Memorial Walk

In September the white camellias that border the Kate Sheppard Memorial Walk are in full bloom. These beautiful, hardy and abundant pure white flowers are more than just attractive harbingers of spring. They are the poignant symbols of the women's suffrage movement in New Zealand, worn by the suffragettes, who also sent them to MPs who supported giving them the vote. When it comes to women's suffrage, tiny New Zealand was a world leader. In September 1893 it became the first self-governing country in the world to award women the right to vote in parliamentary elections. It was a major breakthrough in the fierce battle for women's suffrage which had been raging in Britain for almost three decades. The leader of the New Zealand movement was Kate Sheppard, a pioneer with radical ideas who settled in Christchurch. Always held in high regard, in 1993 the Kate Sheppard Memorial Walk was opened to commemorate her world-altering success. In that year Canterbury women gifted 100 camellias to the Gardens, and these expanded a smaller camellia collection into the Kate Sheppard Memorial Walk. In 1993, a new variety of white camellia, named 'Kate Sheppard', was created to mark the 100th anniversary of the successful campaign. The Memorial Walk is across the Avon River opposite the Hall Lawn, named for Sir John Hall, Premier of New Zealand from 1879 to 1882, who supported votes for women and moved the Bill that gave them the franchise.

The Pond

ABOVE: Trilliums

Magnetic Observatory

In 1901, not far from the conservatories, a magnetic observatory was erected in the Botanic Gardens to assist explorers such as Robert Falcon Scott and Ernest Shackleton with their magnetic surveys in Antarctica. When electric trams were introduced in 1910, the sensitive equipment started to pick up their vibrations. This affected the readings and the magnetic observatory was moved first to Amberley then later to Lauder, with a backup station at Eyrewell.

The buildings were constructed with copper nails and brass screws, locks and hinges to be free from foreign magnetic influence. A wooden building seen beside the Climatological Station is a remnant of the observatory from 1941.

"On a Sunday morning, when my two children were pre-schoolers, I would take them to the Gardens to feed the ducks and enjoy the play area. This helped fill in the day while my husband was skiing at Craigieburn in the days before Mt Hutt."

Pinus patula

Abies pinsapo (Spanish Fir)

Pinetum

To discover the Pinetum is to stumble into a glorious grove of tall, luxuriant, textured needled and coniferous trees, worthy of a fairytale forest.

To discover the pinetum is to stumble into a glorious grove of tall, luxuriant, textured, needled and coniferous trees, worthy of a fairytale forest. On a more prosaic level, the pinetum, which is an arboretum of pines and conifers, was planted for research, education, and display and was started prior to World War II. It was expanded in 1961 when the southern section, which was used as the Botanic Gardens' refuse dump, was cleared and planted with conifers. The Pinetum has matured to include an extensive collection which includes many species and cultivars of cedar (*Cedrus*), cypress (*Cupressus*), fir (*Abies*), larch (*Larix*), juniper (*Juniperus*), pine (*Pinus*) and spruce (*Picea*). It includes several commemorative plantings, including the Bhutan Pine (*Pinus wallichiana*) planted by His Holiness the 24th Dalai Lama of Tibet, the Golden Deodar (*Cedrus deodara* 'Aurea') planted in 1961 to commemorate the opening of the MacGibbon Gates, and the stone pine (*Pinus pinea*) planted in 1963 to commemorate the centenary of the Gardens.

Cunninghamia lanceolata (Chinese Fir)

Fresh, fragrant air, light filtering through spiky needles – the pinetum is an invigorating destination of silence and calm – a wonderful place to end the day and watch the setting sun stretch shadows on the forest floor.

Araucaria araucana (Monkey Puzzle)

Pinus patula

Seasons

© Priscilla Chapman

SPRING

© Liz Clark

© Liz Clark

© Priscilla Chapman

SUMMER

© Liz Clark

AUTUMN

© Liz Clark

© Liz Clark

WINTER

© Jeremy Hawker

Ngāi Tūāhuriri, based north of Christchurch at Tuahiwi, is the Māori tribal authority (Manawhenua) with guardianship (Kaitiakitanga) over this part of the city.

Ngāi Tūāhuriri has a strong interest in waterways protection and enhancement. The Gardens provide a place to strengthen the values associated with the Ngāi Tahu relationship to plants and animals (Mahinga Kai).

The New Botanic Gardens Centre

In December 2012 the Christchurch City Council announced the construction of the new Visitor Centre, on the site where the nursery and offices once stood.

Magnificently designed and built mainly of glass, the distinctive design of the centre is in the spirit of classic garden architecture found in the nearby Cuningham House but with a contemporary twist. The extensive use of glass gives a sense of spaciousness. The building is light and airy, its glass exterior affording views of the surrounding trees and plants.

As a centre for plant production, research and education, the complex houses a herbarium and nursery facilities with greenhouses. There is also a multi-function seminar/education room, a library and archive area, and staff spaces. Of particular interest to leisure visitors, a café replaces the Tea Kiosk (closed following the February 2011 earthquake), making this a hub for meetings and casual get-togethers, a space where families can spend time.

Engrossing exhibitions and exciting interactive displays of the botanical collection can be accessed by the million-plus visitors who flock to the Botanic Gardens in all seasons.

The building was designed by leading architects Patterson Associates, who won a concept design competition in 2009. Local Christchurch firm Leighs Construction won the tender in 2012 to build the project and is responsible for its construction.

The design and placement of the centre allows riverbank and lawn areas to be opened up for visitor enjoyment, creating an idyllic spot for picnics that is also suitable for sculpture, exhibitions and performances.

The construction of the centre gives Botanic Gardens staff improved facilities for research and educational activities. The nursery area, where plants are grown for the grounds and conservatories, is now in view of visitors.

One hundred and fifty years on from the planting of the first oak in 1863, the vision of the Christchurch Botanic Gardens' founders, and the dedicated work of its subsequent curators and caretakers, sees this spectacular expanse flourishing. Offering a unique experience to every visitor, the Gardens provide a place of peace, calm and contemplation. A venue for fun, freedom and frivolity. A location to learn, listen and love; but above all a place of all-encompassing beauty. The Gardens are truly a gift to treasure forever.

The Artist & Photographer

Denise Hunter

Denise Hunter paints because she enjoys the creative process hugely and seems happiest in herself when painting. She lets the idea reveal itself. Like a puzzle it seems to unfold, coming together in front of her with colour and form.

The simple things of seeing light filtering through the water on the shoreline, the clouds swirling against the mountains, all create majestic qualities of Mother Nature that continue to inspire Hunter.

Passionate about colour, contrast, movement and light, Hunter's latest works reflect her love of vivacity found in people and places.

Hunter has won numerous awards and exhibited in many overseas collections including the Broadway Gallery New York in 2012.

Her work continues to evolve.

The *Writers*

Angela Bennett

For Angela Bennett writing has always been one of life's staples. Although a prolific writer from an early age, journalism was not an initial career choice. However after training in pharmacology and enjoying several business management roles, she ventured into making her creative impetus a vocation by taking on a part-time job feature writing. Enamoured by the fascination of the written word, she soon found that journalism took centre stage. She has now been a professional writer and editor for twenty years.

Jacqui Wood

A self-confessed lily freak and grammar vandal, copywriter Jacqui Wood, sees words as pictures.

She attributes this quirk to decades in film and television production and a career devoted to helping some of New Zealand's most impressive producers and directors bring their scripts to life on screen. Her favourite lily is Tī Kōuka (Cordyline australis) and her fervent wish is for a parfumer to truly capture the scent of its exquisite blossoms.

Cynthia Kepple

Cynthia Kepple is a freelance journalist, with a background in news journalism. She has extensive experience in PR, marketing communications, and the hospitality/tourism industry. Her stories and images about places and people have been published in a variety of newspapers and lifestyle and industry magazines. She is currently organiser and presenter of 'All About Gardening', the Canterbury Horticultural Society's flagship programme, and an energetic committee member of the Cashmere Garden Club.

Karin O Donnell

Karin O'Donnell hails from Johannesburg, South Africa. A very eventful working life chasing numerous careers has included more than eight years as an adult education tutor, among other interesting pursuits. Currently she is an employment coach.

She has been a professional writer and editor since 2004, and, although she has worked on a few books in the past, she is particularly pleased to be associated with this one.

Acknowledgements

A special thank you to the following for all their help and support which has been invaluable to produce this book on 'The Botanic Gardens'.

Bruce Bascand, Janice Page and all the great team at The Caxton Press.

John Clemens, Lynda Burns, Sue Molloy, Jeremy Hawker, Bede Nottingham, Richard Poole, David Barwick, Susan Sanders and all the wonderful Christchurch Botanic Garden staff.

My great team of writers, Angela Bennett, Jacqui Wood, Cynthia Kepple, Karin O'Donnell and proof readers Lara O'Donnell and Cathrine Ackroyd.

Additional photography from Priscilla Chapman, Liz Clark and Peter Morath.

The Friends of the Christchurch Botanic Gardens, The Canterbury Museum, Christchurch City Libraries, family and friends.

Publisher's Note

This book showcases so many creative talents. It is also a work which has involved the collaboration of a very positive group of people. It celebrates all those endeavours and of course the wonderful Gardens themselves.

Denise Hunter is so enthusiastic about the Gardens. When she approached us with her concept, we decided to back her that day. Her enthusiasm was infectious, and her talent for photography and painting was apparent.

The other big things were - Denise's decision, from the start, to involve the staff of the Gardens; the support from her team of writers; and from my viewpoint the confidence I have in Janice Page, Art Studio & Prepress Manager at The Caxton Press to beautifully design the book's layout, and our team of world class printers.

We have printed this book in our factory on Victoria Street, in the Christchurch CBD. We lost our historic office building after the September 2010 earthquakes. We have continued to operate in the remaining buildings since further extensive damage in the February 2011 earthquakes. In 2014 we will shift to a new purpose-built factory at Wigram. So while this book principally displays the beautiful photography and art of Denise Hunter, it has also been a pleasure to showcase her work and to celebrate the Gardens in a book entirely designed, printed and published in Christchurch by The Caxton Press.

I thank Denise and also the staff of the Christchurch Botanic Gardens.

Bruce Bascand, Managing Director, The Caxton Press.

Friends of the Christchurch Botanic Gardens

Congratulations to Denise Hunter and The Caxton Press on the production of this book.

It is a long awaited tribute to our beautiful gardens and a significant resource for our visitors
The Friends raise funds for Gardens projects by providing daily and group guided tours and plants for sale.

For further information please go to:
www.friendschchbotanicgardens.org.nz

Part proceeds from the sale of this book will be donated to the Christchurch Botanic Gardens.